THE METAPHYSICAL POETS

Albrecht Dürer, 'Melancholia' (1514)

THE
METAPHYSICAL
POETS

COLLECTOR'S POETRY LIBRARY

This edition first published in 2004 by
COLLECTOR'S POETRY LIBRARY
an imprint of CRW Publishing Limited
69 Gloucester Crescent, London NW1 7EG

ISBN 1 904919 38 3

2 4 6 8 10 9 7 5 3 1

Typeset in Perpetua by Bookcraft Ltd,
Stroud, Gloucestershire, UK

Printed and bound in China by Imago

Contents

Ben Jonson (1573–1637)

Edward, Lord Herbert of Cherbury (1583–1648)

Aurelian Townshend (1583–1643)

Henry King (1592–1669)

Francis Quarles (1592–1644)

George Herbert (1593–1633)

Thomas Carew (1595–1639)

Sir William Davenant (1605–1668)

Edmund Waller (1606–1687)

John Milton (1608–1674)

John Suckling (1609–1642)

El Greco, 'St Veronica With the Sudary' (1579)

Portrait of John Donne

Introduction

But Wit, abstracted from its effects upon the hearer, may be more rigorously and philosophically considered as a kind of discordia concors; a combination of dissimilar images, or discovery of occult resemblances in things apparently unlike. Of wit, thus defined, they have more than enough. The most heterogeneous ideas are yoked by violence together; nature and art are ransacked for illustrations, comparisons, and allusions; their learning instructs, and their subtlety surprises; but the reader commonly thinks his improvement dearly bought, and, though he sometimes admires, is seldom pleased.

Samuel Johnson, describing the Metaphysical
Poets in his *Lives of the Poets* (1779–81)

THE questions most often asked about the Metaphysical poets of the sixteenth and seventeenth centuries are, firstly, who were they, and secondly, why were they called 'Metaphysical'? Neither of these questions is easy to answer. To take the second question first, the application to these writers of the term 'Metaphysical' stems originally from a critical essay by John Dryden, the seventeenth-century Poet Laureate. Dryden complained that John Donne 'affects the metaphysics, not only in his satires, but in his amorous verses, where nature only should reign; and perplexes the minds of the fair sex with nice speculations of philosophy, when he should engage their hearts, and entertain them with the softness of love'. This phrase of Dryden's, 'affecting the metaphysics', was then taken up by others. Dr Johnson, in his *Life of Cowley*, noted that at the beginning of the seventeenth century 'appeared a race of writers that may be termed the metaphysical poets'.

Yet, the Metaphysical poets did not have a manifesto, and although many of its proponents were friends and admirers of one another, their work did not spring from a commonly-articulated belief about what poetry should be. Their 'movement' was, rather, a reaction: a reaction born predominantly from individual writers' dissatisfaction with the ornately stylised poetry and writings of the Tudor period. Elizabethan literature (of which writers such as Edmund Spenser and Sir Philip Sidney are notable proponents) tended to rely on a fairly narrow group of images and poetic symbols – lutes, shepherds, nymphs, and so on – to express and codify its messages. Writers such as John Donne and George Herbert (the two most widely-discussed and representative Metaphysical poets) rebelled against such poetic constraints by using new and unusual metaphors and symbols to express their themes. It is the use of such original and quirky symbols – often called 'conceits' – which really defines Metaphysical poetry.

In his poem 'A Valediction, Forbidding Mourning', Donne employs one of the most famous Metaphysical conceits: comparing himself and his lover to a pair of compasses. He extends this image as far as it will go, using it to discuss the unity and separation of two lovers, as well as the essential oneness-yet-apartness of body and soul. These conceits, then, are not employed merely to make the verse sound more interesting or original. They are introduced as analogies, and then completely interrogated and expanded upon to form the structure of the poem itself.

And Metaphysical poetry is *highly* structural. As well as being strongly emotional, it is markedly intellectual; and at its best it fuses emotion and what Dryden called the 'speculations of philosophy'. This fusion of rigorous thought and complex feeling is given its very shape by the central idea. Herbert, in his most famous poem, 'Easter Wings', takes this shaping-by-conceit to its limit, and actually allows his conceit – that Christ spiritually bears man away with him, as if in flight – to mould the visual image of the verse upon the page: the stanzas form the shape of a pair of outstretched wings.

Another hallmark of Metaphysical poetry (which also distinguishes it from the poetry of the Tudor period) is its unusual verse forms and metrical structures. Ben Jonson famously said that Donne 'deserved hanging' for the way he handled conventional rhythm, and Samuel Johnson noted that the Metaphysicals' poems 'stood the trial of the finger better than of the ear; for the modulation was so imperfect, that they were only found to be verses by counting the syllables'. But Metaphysical verse is not meant to flow perfectly: it is rhythmically unusual because it is trying to do something different. The poets are aiming for a dramatic effect, or they are trying to copy the metre of conversation. Perhaps this is one of the reasons why they have stood the test of time better than more formal poets like Dryden and Johnson. The Metaphysicals' verse sounds much more 'modern' than anything that preceded or followed it.

Another, perhaps less tangible, hallmark of Metaphysical poetry is its Christian devotion. This period of English literature – arguably more so than any other – centres around religious writing and theological interrogation, and many of its greatest writers were clergymen. John Donne (the Dean of St Pauls) deals with God in terms of the human body, writing of death and sexual desire; George Herbert focuses on grace and how to come to a more human understanding of God. Perhaps the technique, which

Johnson identified, of discovering 'occult resemblances in things apparently unlike', is part of this concern: the Metaphysicals and their conceits were striving to draw together the physical and the spiritual, and to find religious connections between seemingly unconnected things.

So who exactly *were* the Metaphysical poets? Some writers – such as Donne, Herbert, Thomas Carew and Henry Vaughan – can clearly be classed as Metaphysical poets because they consistently employ the techniques discussed above and these techniques inform the majority of their work. However, many of the poets represented in this selection might equally well be classed as 'Cavalier Poets' (that is, poets of the English Civil War), or – like Shakespeare and Milton – stand in a class of their own. But their works selected for this book tend to hinge around conceits, to be concerned with God, or to be expressed with a certain quirkiness of style; and for these reasons they may legitimately be called 'Metaphysical'.

Peter Harness

Portrait of George Herbert

Manuscript of George Herbert's poem 'Easter Wings'

THE METAPHYSICAL
POETS

*Be thine own palace, or
the world's thy jail.*

John Donne

Robert Southwell (1561–1595)

LOOK HOME

RETIRED thoughts enjoy their own delights,
As beauty doth in self-beholding eye;
Man's mind a mirror is of heavenly sights,
A brief wherein all marvels summèd lie,
Of fairest forms and sweetest shapes the store,
Most graceful all, yet thought may grace them more.

The mind a creature is, yet can create,
To nature's patterns adding higher skill;
Of finest works with better could the state
If force of wit had equal power of will.
Device of man in working hath no end,
What thought can think, another thought can mend.

Man's soul of endless beauty image is,
Drawn by the work of endless skill and might;
This skillful might gave many sparks of bliss
And, to discern this bliss, a native light;
To frame God's image as his worths required
His might, his skill, his word and will conspired.

All that he had his image should present,
All that it should present it could afford,
To that he could afford his will was bent,
His will was followed with performing word.
Let this suffice, by this conceive the rest, –
He should, he could, he would, he did, the best.

Sir Walter Raleigh (1552–1618)

A FAREWELL TO FALSE LOVE

FAREWELL, false love, the oracle of lies,
A mortal foe and enemy to rest;
An envious boy, from whom all cares arise,
A bastard vile, a beast with rage possessed;
A way of error, a temple full of treason,
In all effects contrary unto reason.

A poisoned serpent covered all with flowers,
Mother of sighs and murderer of repose,
A sea of sorrows whence are drawn such showers
As moisture lend to every grief that grows;
A school of guile, a net of deep deceit,
A gilded hook that holds a poisoned bait.

A fortress foiled, which reason did defend,
A siren song, a fever of the mind,
A maze wherein affection finds no end,
A raging cloud that runs before the wind,
A substance like the shadow of the sun,
A goal of grief for which the wisest run.

A quenchless fire, a nurse of trembling fear,
A path that leads to peril and mishap;
A true retreat of sorrow and despair,
An idle boy that sleeps in pleasure's lap,
A deep distrust of that which certain seems,
A hope of that which reason doubtful deems.

Sith then thy trains my younger years betrayed,
And for my faith ingratitude I find,
And sith repentance hath my wrongs bewrayed,
Whose course was ever contrary to kind –
False love, desire, and beauty frail, adieu!
Dead is the root whence all these fancies grew.

THE PASSIONATE MAN'S PILGRIMAGE

GIVE me my scallop shell of quiet,
My staff of faith to walk upon,
My scrip of joy, immortal diet,
My bottle of salvation,
My gown of glory, hope's true gage,
And thus I'll take my pilgrimage.

Blood must be my body's balmer,
No other balm will there be given,
Whilst my soul, like a white palmer,
Travels to the land of heaven;
Over the silver mountains,
Where spring the nectar fountains;
And there I'll kiss
The bowl of bliss,
And drink my eternal fill
On every milken hill.
My soul will be a-dry before,
But after it will ne'er thirst more.

And by the happy blissful way
More peaceful pilgrims I shall see,
That have shook off their gowns of clay,
And go apparelled fresh like me.
I'll bring them first
To slake their thirst,
And then to taste those nectar suckets,
At the clear wells
Where sweetness dwells,
Drawn up by saints in crystal buckets.
And when our bottles and all we
Are fill'd with immortality,
Then the holy paths we'll travel,
Strew'd with rubies thick as gravel,
Ceilings of diamonds, sapphire floors,
High walls of coral, and pearl bowers.

From thence to heaven's bribeless hall
Where no corrupted voices brawl,
No conscience molten into gold,
Nor forg'd accusers bought and sold,
No cause deferred, nor vain-spent journey,
For there Christ is the king's attorney,
Who pleads for all without degrees,
And he hath angels, but no fees.

When the grand twelve million jury
Of our sins and sinful fury,
'Gainst our souls black verdicts give,
Christ pleads his death, and then we live.
Be thou my speaker, taintless pleader,
Unblotted lawyer, true proceeder,
Thou movest salvation even for alms,
Not with a bribed lawyer's palms.

And this is my eternal plea
To him that made heaven, earth, and sea,
Seeing my flesh must die so soon,
And want a head to dine next noon,
Just at the stroke when my veins start and spread,
Set on my soul an everlasting head.
Then am I ready, like a palmer fit,
To tread those blest paths which before I writ.

William Shakespeare (1564–1616)

THE PASSIONATE PILGRIM (1)

WHEN my love swears that she is made of truth,
I do believe her, though I know she lies,
That she might think me some untutor'd youth,
Unskilful in the world's false forgeries.
Thus vainly thinking that she thinks me young,
Although I know my years be past the best,
I smiling credit her false-speaking tongue,
Outfacing faults in love with love's ill rest.
But wherefore says my love that she is young?
And wherefore say not I that I am old?
O, love's best habit is a soothing tongue,
And age, in love, loves not to have years told.
Therefore I'll lie with love, and love with me,
Since that our faults in love thus smothered be.

THE PASSIONATE PILGRIM (2)

Two loves I have, of comfort and despair,
That like two spirits do suggest me still;
My better angel is a man right fair,
My worser spirit a woman coloured ill.
To win me soon to hell, my female evil
Tempteth my better angel from my side,
And would corrupt my saint to be a devil,
Wooing his purity with her fair pride.
And whether that my angel be turned fiend,
Suspect I may, yet not directly tell:
For being both to me, both to each friend,
I guess one angel in another's hell;
The truth I shall not know, but live in doubt,
Till my bad angel fire my good one out.

THE PASSIONATE PILGRIM (7)

Fair is my love, but not so fair as fickle;
Mild as a dove, but neither true nor trusty;
Brighter than glass, and yet, as glass is, brittle;
Softer than wax, and yet, as iron, rusty:
A lily pale, with damask dye to grace her,
None fairer, nor none falser to deface her.

Her lips to mine how often hath she joined,
Between each kiss her oaths of true love swearing!
How many tales to please me hath she coined,
Dreading my love, the loss thereof still fearing!
Yet in the midst of all her pure protestings,
Her faith, her oaths, her tears, and all were jestings.

She burned with love, as straw with fire flameth;
She burned out love, as soon as straw outburneth;
She framed the love, and yet she foiled the framing;
She bade love last, and yet she fell a-turning.
Was this a lover, or a lecher whether?
Bad in the best, though excellent in neither.

THE PASSIONATE PILGRIM (13)

BEAUTY is but a vain and doubtful good;
A shining gloss that fadeth suddenly;
A flower that dies when first it gins to bud;
A brittle glass that's broken presently:
A doubtful good, a gloss, a glass, a flower,
Lost, faded, broken, dead within an hour.

And as goods lost are seld or never found,
As faded gloss no rubbing will refresh,
As flowers dead lie withered on the ground,
As broken glass no cement can redress,
So beauty blemished once for ever lost,
In spite of physic, painting, pain and cost.

SONNET 130

My mistress' eyes are nothing like the sun;
Coral is far more red than her lips' red;
If snow be white, why then her breasts are dun;
If hairs be wires, black wires grow on her head.
I have seen roses damasked, red and white,
But no such roses see I in her cheeks;
And in some perfumes is there more delight
Than in the breath that from my mistress reeks.
I love to hear her speak, yet well I know
That music hath a far more pleasing sound;
I grant I never saw a goddess go;
My mistress, when she walks, treads on the ground:
    And yet, by heaven, I think my love as rare
    As any she belied with false compare.

Sir Henry Wotton (1568–1639)

A Hymn to My God

IN A NIGHT OF MY LATE SICKNESSE

O H thou great Power, in whom I move,
  For whom I live, to whom I die,
Behold me through thy beams of love,
  Whilst on this Couch of tears I lie;
And Cleanse my sordid soul within,
By thy Christs Blood, the bath of sin.

No hallowed oils, no grains I need,
  No rags of Saints, no purging fire,
One rosy drop from David's Seed
  Was worlds of seas, to quench thine Ire.
O precious Ransom! which once paid,
That *Consummatum est* was said.

And said by him, that said no more,
  But seal'd it with his sacred breath.
Thou then, that hast dispung'd my score,
  And dying, wast the death of Death;
Be to me now, on thee I call,
My Life, my Strength, my Joy, my All.

John Donne (1572–1631)

A Hymn to God the Father

WILT thou forgive that sin where I begun,
   Which is my sin, though it were done before?
Wilt thou forgive that sin, through which I run,
   And do run still, though still I do deplore?
      When thou hast done, thou hast not done,
       For I have more.

Wilt thou forgive that sin which I have won
   Others to sin, and made my sin their door?
Wilt thou forgive that sin which I did shun
   A year or two, but wallowed in, a score?
      When thou hast done, thou hast not done,
       For I have more.

I have a sin of fear, that when I have spun
   My last thread, I shall perish on the shore;
But swear by thyself, that at my death thy Son
   Shall shine as he shines now, and heretofore;
      And, having done that, thou hast done;
       I fear no more.

A Nocturnal Upon St Lucie's Day

BEING THE SHORTEST DAY

'Tis the year's midnight, and it is the day's,
    Lucy's, who scarce seven hours herself unmasks;
    The sun is spent, and now his flasks
    Send forth light squibs, no constant rays;
        The world's whole sap is sunk:
The general balm th'hydroptic earth hath drunk,
Whither, as to the bed's-feet, life is shrunk,
Dead and interred; yet all these seem to laugh,
Compared with me, who am their epitaph.

Study me then, you who shall lovers be
At the next world, that is, at the next spring;
    For I am every dead thing,
    In whom Love wrought new alchemy.
        For his art did express
A quintessence even from nothingness,
From dull privations, and lean emptiness:
He ruined me, and I am re-begot
Of absence, darkness, death – things which are not.

All others, from all things, draw all that's good,
Life, soul, form, spirit, whence they being have;
    I, by Love's limbec, am the grave
    Of all, that's nothing. Oft a flood
        Have we two wept, and so
Drowned the whole world, us two; oft did we grow
To be two chaoses, when we did show
Care to aught else; and often absences
Withdrew our souls, and made us carcasses.

But I am by her death – which word wrongs her –
Of the first nothing, the elixir grown;
　　Were I a man, that I were one,
　　I needs must know; I should prefer,
　　　　If I were any beast,
Some ends, some means; yea plants, yea stones detest,
And love; all, all some properties invest.
If I an ordinary nothing were,
As shadow, a light, and body must be here.

But I am none; nor will my sun renew.
You lovers, for whose sake the lesser sun
　　At this time to the Goat is run
　　To fetch new lust, and give it you,
　　　　Enjoy your summer all,
Since she enjoys her long night's festival.
Let me prepare towards her, and let me call
This hour her vigil, and her eve, since this
Both the year's and the day's deep midnight is.

ON HIS MISTRESS

BY our first strange and fatal interview,
By all desires which thereof did ensue,
By our long starving hopes, by that remorse
Which my words masculine persuasive force
Begot in thee, and by the memory
Of hurts, which spies and rivals threatened me,
I calmly beg. But by thy father's wrath,
By all pains, which want and divorcement hath,
I conjure thee, and all the oaths which I
And thou have sworn to seal joint constancy,
Here I unswear, and overswear them thus;
Thou shalt not love by ways so dangerous.
Temper, O fair love, love's impetuous rage;
Be my true mistress still, not my feigned page.
I'll go, and, by thy kind leave, leave behind
Thee, only worthy to nurse in my mind
Thirst to come back; O! if thou die before,
My soul from other lands to thee shall soar.
Thy else almighty beauty cannot move
Rage from the seas, nor thy love teach them love,
Nor tame wild Boreas' harshness; thou hast read
How roughly he in pieces shivered
Fair Orithea, whom he swore he loved.
Fall ill or good, 'tis madness to have proved
Dangers unurged; feed on this flattery,
That absent lovers one in th'other be.
Dissemble nothing, not a boy, nor change
Thy body's habit, nor mind; be not strange
To thyself only. All will spy in thy face
A blushing womanly discovering grace.

Richly clothed apes are called apes, and as soon
Eclipsed as bright, we call the moon the moon.
Men of France, changeable chameleons,
Spitals of diseases, shops of fashions,
Love's fuellers, and the rightest company
Of players, which upon the world's stage be,
Will quickly know thee, and no less, alas!
Th'indifferent Italian, as we pass
His warm land, well content to think thee page,
Will hunt thee with such lust, and hideous rage,
As Lot's fair guests were vexed. But none of these
Nor spongy hydroptic Dutch shall thee displease,
If thou stay here. O stay here, for, for thee
England is only a worthy gallery,
To walk in expectation, till from thence
Our greatest king call thee to his presence.
When I am gone, dream me some happiness;
Nor let thy looks our long-hid love confess;
Nor praise, nor dispraise me, nor bless nor curse
Openly love's force, nor in bed fright thy nurse
With midnight's startings, crying out, O! O!
Nurse, O! my love is slain; I saw him go
O'er the white Alps alone; I saw him, I,
Assailed, fight, taken, stabbed, bleed, fall, and die.
Augur me better chance, except dread Jove
Think it enough for me to have had thy love.

ON HIMSELF

My fortune and my choice this custom break,
   When we are speechless grown
                             to make stones speak.
Though no stone tell thee what I was, yet thou
In my grave's inside seest what thou art now:
Yet thou'rt not yet so good; till death us lay
To ripe and mellow here, we're stubborn clay.
Parents make us earth, and souls dignify
Us to be glass; here to grow gold we lie.
Whilst in our souls sin bred and pampered is,
Our souls become worm-eaten carcasses,
So we ourselves miraculously destroy.
Here bodies with less miracle enjoy
Such privileges, enabled here to scale
Heaven, when the trumpet's air shall them exhale.
Hear this, and mend thyself, and thou mend'st me,
By making me, being dead, do good to thee;
   And think me well composed, that I could now
   A last sick hour to syllables allow.

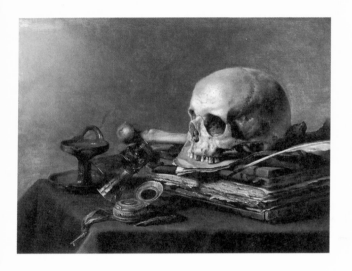

Pieter Claesz, 'Vanitas Still Life'

THE WILL

BEFORE I sigh my last gasp, let me breathe,
Great Love, some legacies; I here bequeath
Mine eyes to Argus, if mine eyes can see;
If they be blind, then, Love, I give them thee;
My tongue to Fame; to ambassadors mine ears;
     To women, or the sea, my tears.
    Thou, Love, hast taught me heretofore
  By making me serve her who had twenty more,
That I should give to none,
                but such as had too much before.

My constancy I to the planets give;
My truth to them who at the court do live;
My ingenuity and openness,
To Jesuits; to buffoons my pensiveness;
My silence to any, who abroad hath been;
     My money to a Capuchin.
    Thou, Love, taught'st me, by appointing me
  To love there, where no love received can be,
Only to give to such as have an incapacity.

My faith I give to Roman Catholics;
All my good works unto the Schismatics
Of Amsterdam; my best civility
And courtship to an University;
My modesty I give to soldiers bare;
     My patience let gamesters share.
    Thou, Love, taught'st me, by making me
  Love her that holds my love disparity,
Only to give to those that count my gifts indignity.

I give my reputation to those
Which were my friends; mine industry to foes;
To schoolmen I bequeath my doubtfulness;
My sickness to physicians, or excess;
To nature all that I in rhyme have writ;
     And to my company my wit.
   Thou, Love, by making me adore
Her, who begot this love in me before,
Taught'st me to make, as though I gave,
               when I do but restore.

To him for whom the passing-bell next tolls,
I give my physic books; my written rolls
Of moral counsels I to Bedlam give;
My brazen medals unto them which live
In want of bread; to them which pass among
     All foreigners, mine English tongue.
   Thou, Love, by making me love one
Who thinks her friendship a fit portion
For younger lovers, dost my gifts thus disproportion.

Therefore I'll give no more, but I'll undo
The world by dying, because love dies too.
Then all your beauties will be no more worth
Than gold in mines, where none doth draw it forth;
And all your graces no more use shall have,
     Than a sun-dial in a grave.
   Thou, Love, taught'st me by making me
Love her, who doth neglect both me and thee,
To invent, and practise this one way,
               to annihilate all three.

THE ANNIVERSARY

ALL kings, and all their favourites,
   All glory of honours, beauties, wits,
The sun itself, which makes times, as they pass,
Is elder by a year now than it was
When thou and I first one another saw.
All other things to their destruction draw,
   Only our love hath no decay;
This no tomorrow hath, nor yesterday;
Running it never runs from us away,
But truly keeps his first, last, everlasting day.

   Two graves must hide thine and my corse;
    If one might, death were no divorce.
Alas! as well as other princes, we
– Who prince enough in one another be –
Must leave at last in death these eyes and ears,
Oft fed with true oaths, and with sweet salt tears;
   But souls where nothing dwells but love
– All other thoughts being inmates – then shall prove
This or a love increasèd there above,
When bodies to their graves,

               souls from their graves remove.

And then we shall be throughly blest;
  But we no more than all the rest.
Here upon earth we're kings, and none but we
Can be such kings, nor of such subjects be.
Who is so safe as we? where none can do
Treason to us, except one of us two.
  True and false fears let us refrain,
Let us love nobly, and live, and add again
Years and years unto years, till we attain
To write threescore; this is the second of our reign.

THE BLOSSOM

L ITTLE think'st thou, poor flower,
  Whom I've watch'd six or seven days,
And seen thy birth, and seen what every hour
Gave to thy growth, thee to this height to raise,
And now dost laugh and triumph on this bough:
    Little think'st thou,
That it will freeze anon, and that I shall
Tomorrow find thee fallen, or not at all.

  Little think'st thou, poor heart,
  That labourest yet to nestle thee,
And think'st by hovering here to get a part
In a forbidden or forbidding tree,
And hopest her stiffness by long siege to bow:
    Little think'st thou
That thou tomorrow, ere the sun doth wake,
Must with the sun and me a journey take.

But thou, which lovest to be
  Subtle to plague thyself, wilt say,
Alas! if you must go, what's that to me?
Here lies my business, and here I will stay:
You go to friends, whose love and means present
    Various content
To your eyes, ears, and taste, and every part;
If then your body go, what need your heart?

  Well then, stay here; but know,
  When thou hast stayed and done thy most,
A naked thinking heart, that makes no show,
Is to a woman but a kind of ghost.
How shall she know my heart; or having none,
    Know thee for one?
Practice may make her know some other part;
But take my word, she doth not know a heart.

  Meet me in London, then,
  Twenty days hence, and thou shalt see
Me fresher and more fat, by being with men,
Than if I had stayed still with her and thee.
For God's sake, if you can, be you so too;
    I will give you
There to another friend, whom we shall find
As glad to have my body as my mind.

THE EXPIRATION

So, so, break off this last lamenting kiss,
  Which sucks two souls, and vapours both away;
Turn thou ghost that way, and let me turn this,
    And let ourselves benight our happiest day;
We ask none leave to love; nor will we owe
    Any, so cheap a death, as saying, Go.

Go; and if that word have not quite killed thee,
  Ease me with death, by bidding me go too.
Oh, if it have, let my word work on me,
    And a just office on a murderer do.
Except it be too late, to kill me so,
    Being double dead, going, and bidding, go.

THE FLEA

MARK but this flea, and mark in this,
  How little that which thou deniest me is;
It suck'd me first, and now sucks thee,
And in this flea our two bloods mingled be.
Thou know'st that this cannot be said
A sin, nor shame, nor loss of maidenhead;
  Yet this enjoys before it woo,
  And pampered swells with one blood made of two;
  And this, alas! is more than we would do.

O stay, three lives in one flea spare,
Where we almost, yea, more than married are.
This flea is you and I, and this
Our marriage bed, and marriage temple is.
Though parents grudge, and you, we're met,
And cloistered in these living walls of jet.
  Though use make you apt to kill me,
  Let not to that self-murder added be,
  And sacrilege, three sins in killing three.

Cruel and sudden, hast thou since
Purpled thy nail in blood of innocence?
Wherein could this flea guilty be,
Except in that drop which it sucked from thee?
Yet thou triumph'st, and say'st that thou
Find'st not thyself nor me the weaker now.
  'Tis true; then learn how false fears be;
  Just so much honour, when thou yield'st to me,
  Will waste, as this flea's death took life from thee.

THE GOOD-MORROW

I WONDER by my troth, what thou and I
Did, till we loved? were we not weaned till then?
But sucked on country pleasures, childishly?
Or snorted we in the Seven Sleepers' den?
'Twas so; but this, all pleasures fancies be.
If ever any beauty I did see,
Which I desired, and got, 'twas but a dream of thee.

And now good-morrow to our waking souls,
Which watch not one another out of fear;
For love all love of other sights controls,
And makes one little room an everywhere.
Let sea-discoverers to new worlds have gone;
Let maps to other, worlds on worlds have shown;
Let us possess one world; each hath one, and is one.

My face in thine eye, thine in mine appears,
And true plain hearts do in the faces rest;
Where can we find two better hemispheres
Without sharp north, without declining west?
Whatever dies, was not mixed equally;
If our two loves be one, or thou and I
Love so alike that none can slacken, none can die.

SONG

Go and catch a falling star,
Get with child a mandrake root,
Tell me where all past years are,
Or who cleft the devil's foot,
Teach me to hear mermaids singing,
Or to keep off envy's stinging,
     And find
     What wind
Serves to advance an honest mind.

If thou be'st born to strange sights,
Things invisible to see,
Ride ten thousand days and nights,
Till age snow white hairs on thee,
Thou, when thou return'st, wilt tell me,
All strange wonders that befell thee,
     And swear,
     No where
Lives a woman true and fair.

If thou find'st one, let me know,
Such a pilgrimage were sweet;
Yet do not, I would not go,
Though at next door we might meet,
Though she were true, when you met her,
And last, till you write your letter,
     Yet she
     Will be
False, ere I come, to two, or three.

Woman's Constancy

Now thou hast loved me one whole day,
   Tomorrow when thou leavest, what wilt thou say?
Wilt thou then antedate some new-made vow?
   Or say that now
We are not just those persons which we were?
Or that oaths made in reverential fear
Of Love, and his wrath, any may forswear?
Or, as true deaths true marriages untie,
So lovers' contracts, images of those,
Bind but till sleep, death's image, them unloose?
   Or, your own end to justify,
For having purposed change and falsehood, you
Can have no way but falsehood to be true?
Vain lunatic, against these 'scapes I could
   Dispute, and conquer, if I would;
   Which I abstain to do,
For by tomorrow I may think so too.

The Sun Rising

Busy old fool, unruly Sun,
　　Why dost thou thus,
Through windows, and through curtains, call on us?
Must to thy motions lovers' seasons run?
　　Saucy, pedantic wretch, go chide
　　Late school-boys and sour prentices,
　Go tell court-huntsmen that the king will ride,
　Call country ants to harvest offices;
Love, all alike, no season knows nor clime,
Nor hours, days, months, which are the rags of time.

　　Thy beams so reverend, and strong
　　Why shouldst thou think?
I could eclipse and cloud them with a wink,
But that I would not lose her sight so long.
　　If her eyes have not blinded thine,
　　Look, and tomorrow late tell me,
　Whether both th'Indias of spice and mine
　Be where thou left'st them, or lie here with me.
Ask for those kings whom thou saw'st yesterday,
And thou shalt hear, 'All here in one bed lay.'

　　She's all states, and all princes I;
　　Nothing else is.
Princes do but play us; compared to this,
All honour's mimic, all wealth alchemy.
　　Thou, Sun, art half as happy as we,
　　In that the world's contracted thus;
　Thine age asks ease, and since thy duties be
　To warm the world, that's done in warming us.
Shine here to us, and thou art everywhere;
This bed thy centre is, these walls thy sphere.

Nicholas Poussin, 'Selene and Endymion' (*c.* 1630)

THE CANONISATION

For God's sake hold your tongue, and let me love;
   Or chide my palsy, or my gout;
     My five gray hairs, or ruin'd fortune flout;
With wealth your state, your mind with arts improve;
       Take you a course, get you a place,
       Observe his honour, or his grace;
Or the king's real, or his stamped face
    Contemplate; what you will, approve,
    So you will let me love.

Alas! alas! who's injured by my love?
    What merchant's ships have my sighs drowned?
    Who says my tears have overflow'd his ground?
When did my colds a forward spring remove?
      When did the heats which my veins fill
      Add one more to the plague bill?
Soldiers find wars, and lawyers find out still
    Litigious men, which quarrels move,
    Though she and I do love.

Call's what you will, we are made such by love;
    Call her one, me another fly,
    We're tapers too, and at our own cost die,
And we in us find th'eagle and the dove.
      The phoenix riddle hath more wit
      By us; we two being one, are it.
So, to one neutral thing both sexes fit,
    We die and rise the same, and prove
    Mysterious by this love.

We can die by it, if not live by love,
    And if unfit for tomb or hearse
    Our legend be, it will be fit for verse;
And if no piece of chronicle we prove,
       We'll build in sonnets pretty rooms;
       As well a well-wrought urn becomes
The greatest ashes, as half-acre tombs,
    And by these hymns, all shall approve
    Us canonised for love.

And thus invoke us, 'You, whom reverend love
    Made one another's hermitage;
    You, to whom love was peace, that now is rage;
Who did the whole world's soul contract, and drove
       Into the glasses of your eyes;
       So made such mirrors, and such spies,
That they did all to you epitomise –
    Countries, towns, courts beg from above
    A pattern of your love.'

SONG

SWEETEST love, I do not go,
  For weariness of thee,
Nor in hope the world can show
    A fitter love for me;
      But since that I
At the last must part, 'tis best,
Thus to use myself in jest
    By feigned deaths to die.

Yesternight the sun went hence,
    And yet is here to-day;
He hath no desire nor sense,
    Nor half so short a way;
      Then fear not me,
But believe that I shall make
Speedier journeys, since I take
    More wings and spurs than he.

O how feeble is man's power,
    That if good fortune fall,
Cannot add another hour,
    Nor a lost hour recall;
      But come bad chance,
And we join to it our strength,
And we teach it art and length,
    Itself o'er us to advance.

When thou sigh'st, thou sigh'st not wind,
    But sigh'st my soul away;
When thou weep'st, unkindly kind,
    My life's blood doth decay.
       It cannot be
That thou lovest me as thou say'st,
If in thine my life thou waste,
    That art the best of me.

Let not thy divining heart
    Forethink me any ill;
Destiny may take thy part,
    And may thy fears fulfil.
      But think that we
Are but turned aside to sleep;
They who one another keep
    Alive, ne'er parted be.

AIR AND ANGELS

TWICE or thrice had I loved thee,
  Before I knew thy face or name;
 So in a voice, so in a shapeless flame,
Angels affect us oft, and worshipped be.
  Still when, to where thou wert, I came,
Some lovely glorious nothing did I see.
  But since my soul, whose child love is,
Takes limbs of flesh, and else could nothing do,
  More subtle than the parent is,
Love must not be, but take a body too;
  And therefore what thou wert, and who,
    I bid Love ask, and now
That it assume thy body, I allow,
And fix itself in thy lip, eye, and brow.

Whilst thus to ballast love I thought,
  And so more steadily to have gone,
  With wares which would sink admiration,
I saw I had love's pinnace overfraught;
  Thy every hair for love to work upon
Is much too much; some fitter must be sought;
  For, nor in nothing, nor in things
Extreme, and scattering bright, can love inhere;
  Then as an angel, face and wings
Of air, not pure as it, yet pure doth wear,
  So thy love may be my love's sphere;
    Just such disparity
As is 'twixt air's and angels' purity,
'Twixt women's love, and men's, will ever be.

LOVE'S GROWTH

I SCARCE believe my love to be so pure
    As I had thought it was,
    Because it doth endure
Vicissitude, and season, as the grass;
Methinks I lied all winter, when I swore
My love was infinite, if spring make it more.

But if this medicine, love, which cures all sorrow
    With more, not only be no quintessence,
    But mixed of all stuffs, vexing soul, or sense,
And of the sun his active vigour borrow,
Love's not so pure, and abstract as they use
To say, which have no mistress but their Muse;
But as all else, being elemented too,
Love sometimes would contemplate, sometimes do.

And yet no greater, but more eminent,
    Love by the spring is grown;
    As in the firmament,
Stars by the sun are not enlarged, but shown,
Gentle love deeds, as blossoms on a bough,
From love's awakened root do bud out now.

If, as in water stirred more circles be
    Produced by one, love such additions take,
    Those like so many spheres but one heaven make,
For they are all concentric unto thee;
And though each spring do add to love new heat,
As princes do in times of action get
New taxes, and remit them not in peace,
No winter shall abate this spring's increase.

LOVE'S EXCHANGE

Love, any devil else but you
   Would for a given soul give something too.
At court your fellows every day
Give th'art of rhyming, huntsmanship, or play,
For them which were their own before;
Only I have nothing, which gave more,
But am, alas! by being lowly, lower.

I ask no dispensation now,
To falsify a tear, or sigh, or vow;
I do not sue from thee to draw
A *non obstante* on nature's law;
These are prerogatives, they inhere
In thee and thine; none should forswear
Except that he Love's minion were.

Give me thy weakness, make me blind,
Both ways, as thou and thine, in eyes and mind;
Love, let me never know that this
Is Love, or, that Love childish is;
Let me not know that others know
That she knows my paines, lest that so
A tender shame make me mine own new woe.

If thou give nothing, yet thou'rt just,
Because I would not thy first motions trust;
Small towns which stand stiff, till great shot
Enforce them, by war's law condition not;
Such in Love's warfare is my case;
I may not article for grace,
Having put Love at last to show this face.

This face, by which he could command
And change th'idolatry of any land,
This face, which, wheresoe'er it comes,
Can call vowed men from cloisters, dead from tombs,
And melt both poles at once, and store
Deserts with cities, and make more
Mines in the earth, than quarries were before.

For this, Love is enraged with me,
Yet kills not. If I must example be
To future rebels, if th'unborn
Must learn by my being cut up and torn,
Kill, and dissect me, Love; for this
Torture against thine own end is;
Racked carcasses make ill anatomies.

LOVE'S ALCHEMY

Some that have deeper digged love's mine than I,
Say, where his centric happiness doth lie.
        I have loved, and got, and told,
But should I love, get, tell, till I were old,
I should not find that hidden mystery.
        O! 'tis imposture all;
And as no chemic yet th'elixir got,
        But glorifies his pregnant pot,
        If by the way to him befall
Some odoriferous thing, or medicinal,
    So, lovers dream a rich and long delight,
    But get a winter-seeming summer's night.

Our ease, our thrift, our honour, and our day,
Shall we for this vain bubble's shadow pay?
        Ends love in this, that my man
Can be as happy as I can, if he can
Endure the short scorn of a bridegroom's play?
        That loving wretch that swears,
'Tis not the bodies marry, but the minds,
        Which he in her angelic finds,
        Would swear as justly, that he hears,
In that day's rude hoarse minstrelsy, the spheres.
    Hope not for mind in women; at their best,
    Sweetness and wit they are, but mummy, possessed.

THE APPARITION

WHEN by thy scorn, O murd'ress, I am dead,
    And that thou thinkst thee free
From all solicitation from me,
Then shall my ghost come to thy bed,
And thee, feigned vestal, in worse arms shall see:
Then thy sick taper will begin to wink,
And he, whose thou art then, being tired before,
Will, if thou stir, or pinch to wake him, think
    Thou call'st for more,
And, in false sleep, will from thee shrink,
And then, poor aspen wretch, neglected thou
Bathed in a cold quicksilver sweat wilt lie,
    A verier ghost than I.
What I will say, I will not tell thee now,
Lest that preserve thee; and since my love is spent,
I'd rather thou shouldst painfully repent,
Than by my threatenings rest still innocent.

THE BROKEN HEART

HE is stark mad, whoever says,
  That he hath been in love an hour,
Yet not that love so soon decays,
  But that it can ten in less space devour;
Who will believe me, if I swear
That I have had the plague a year?
  Who would not laugh at me, if I should say,
  I saw a flash of powder burn a day?

Ah, what a trifle is a heart,
  If once into love's hands it come!
All other griefs allow a part
  To other griefs, and ask themselves but some;
They come to us, but us love draws;
He swallows us and never chaws;
  By him, as by chained shot, whole ranks do die;
  He is the tyrant pike, our hearts the fry.

If' 'twere not so, what did become
  Of my heart when I first saw thee?
I brought a heart into the room,
  But from the room I carried none with me.
If it had gone to thee, I know
Mine would have taught thine heart to show
  More pity unto me; but Love, alas!
  At one first blow did shiver it as glass.

Yet nothing can to nothing fall,
    Nor any place be empty quite;
Therefore I think my breast hath all
    Those pieces still, though they be not unite;
And now, as broken glasses show
A hundred lesser faces, so
    My rags of heart can like, wish, and adore,
    But after one such love, can love no more.

A Valediction: Forbidding Mourning

As virtuous men pass mildly away,
    And whisper to their souls to go,
Whilst some of their sad friends do say,
    'Now his breath goes,' and some say, 'No.'

So let us melt, and make no noise,
    No tear-floods, nor sigh-tempests move;
'Twere profanation of our joys
    To tell the laity our love.

Moving of th'earth brings harms and fears;
    Men reckon what it did, and meant;
But trepidation of the spheres,
    Though greater far, is innocent.

Dull sublunary lovers' love
    — Whose soul is sense — cannot admit
Absence, 'cause it doth remove
    The thing which elemented it.

But we by a love so much refined,
    That ourselves know not what it is,
Inter-assurèd of the mind,
    Care less, eyes, lips and hands to miss.

Our two souls therefore, which are one,
    Though I must go, endure not yet
A breach, but an expansion,
    Like gold to aery thinness beat.

If they be two, they are two so
    As stiff twin compasses are two;
Thy soul, the fixed foot, makes no show
    To move, but doth, if th'other do.

And though it in the centre sit,
    Yet, when the other far doth roam,
It leans, and hearkens after it,
    And grows erect, as that comes home.

Such wilt thou be to me, who must,
    Like th'other foot, obliquely run;
Thy firmness makes my circle just,
    And makes me end where I begun.

THE FUNERAL

WHOEVER comes to shroud me, do not harm,
    Nor question much,
That subtle wreath of hair, which crowns my arm;
The mystery, the sign, you must not touch,
    For 'tis my outward soul,
Viceroy to that, which then to heaven being gone,
    Will leave this to control,
And keep these limbs, her provinces, from dissolution.

For if the sinewy thread my brain lets fall
    Through every part
Can tie those parts, and make me one of all,
Those hairs which upward grew, and strength and art
    Have from a better brain,
Can better do't; except she meant that I
    By this should know my pain,
As prisoners then are manacled,
                    when they're condemned to die.

Whate'er she meant by it, bury it with me,
    For since I am
Love's martyr, it might breed idolatry,
If into others' hands these relics came.
    As 'twas humility
To afford to it all that a soul can do,
    So 'tis some bravery,
That since you would have none of me,
                    I bury some of you.

SELF-LOVE

H E that cannot choose but love,
And strives against it still,
Never shall my fancy move,
For he loves against his will;
Nor he which is all his own,
And can at pleasure choose,
When I am caught he can be gone,
And when he list refuse.
Nor he that loves none but fair,
For such by all are sought;
Nor he that can for foul ones care,
For his judgment then is nought;
Nor he that hath wit, for he
Will make me his jest or slave;
Nor a fool, for when others –
He can neither –
Nor he that still his mistress pays,
For she is thralled therefore,
Nor he that pays not, for he says
Within, she's worth no more.
Is there then no kind of men
Whom I may freely prove?
I will vent that humour then
In mine own self-love.

HIS PICTURE

HERE take my picture; though I bid farewell,
Thine, in my heart, where my soul dwells,
                                        shall dwell.
'Tis like me now, but I dead, 'twill be more
When we are shadows both, than 'twas before.
When weatherbeaten I come back; my hand,
Perhaps with rude oars torn, or sun-beams tanned,
My face and breast of haircloth, and my head
With care's rash sudden storms being o'erspread,
My body a sack of bones, broken within,
And powder's blue stains scattered on my skin;
If rival fools tax thee to have loved a man,
So foul and coarse, as, O! I may seem then,
This shall say what I was; and thou shalt say,
'Do his hurts reach me? doth my worth decay?
Or do they reach his judging mind, that he
Should now love less, what he did love to see?
That which in him was fair and delicate,
Was but the milk, which in love's childish state
Did nurse it; who now is grown strong enough
To feed on that, which to disused tastes seems tough.'

HOLY SONNET 1

THOU hast made me, and shall Thy work decay?
Repair me now, for now mine end doth haste;
I run to death, and Death meets me as fast,
And all my pleasures are like yesterday.
I dare not move my dim eyes any way,
Despair behind, and Death before doth cast
Such terror, and my feeble flesh doth waste
By sin in it, which it towards hell doth weigh.
Only Thou art above, and when towards Thee
By Thy leave I can look, I rise again;
But our old subtle foe so tempteth me,
That not one hour myself I can sustain.
Thy grace may wing me to prevent his art,
And Thou like adamant draw mine iron heart.

HOLY SONNET 6

THIS is my play's last scene, here heavens appoint
My pilgrimages last mile; and my race
Idly, yet quickly run, hath this last pace,
My spans last inch, my minutes latest point,
And gluttonous death, will instantly unjoint
My body, and soul, and I shall sleep a space,
But my ever-waking part shall see that face,
Whose fear already shakes my every joint;
Then, as my soul, to heaven her first seat, takes flight,
And earth-borne body, in the earth shall dwell,
So, fall my sins, that all may have their right,
To where they're bred, and would press me, to hell.
Impute me righteous, thus purged of evil,
For thus I leave the world, the flesh, the devil.

HOLY SONNET 7

A T the round earth's imagined corners blow
Your trumpets, angels, and arise, arise
From death, you numberless infinities
Of souls, and to your scattered bodies go;
All whom the flood did, and fire shall o'erthrow,
All whom war, dearth, age, agues, tyrannies,
Despair, law, chance, hath slain, and you, whose eyes
Shall behold God, and never taste death's woe.
But let them sleep, Lord, and me mourn a space,
For, if above all these, my sins abound,
'Tis late to ask abundance of Thy grace,
When we are there. Here on this lowly ground,
Teach me how to repent, for that's as good
As if Thou hadst sealed my pardon with Thy blood.

HOLY SONNET 9

I F poisonous minerals, and if that tree,
Whose fruit threw death on else immortal us,
If lecherous goats, if serpents envious
Cannot be damned, alas! why should I be?
Why should intent or reason, born in me,
Make sins, else equal, in me more heinous?
And, mercy being easy, and glorious
To God; in His stern wrath, why threatens He?
But who am I, that dare dispute with Thee
O God? O! of Thine only worthy blood,
And my tears, make a heavenly Lethean flood,
And drown in it my sin's black memory;
That Thou remember them, some claim as debt,
I think it mercy if Thou wilt forget.

HOLY SONNET 14

BATTER my heart, three-personed God; for you
As yet but knock, breathe, shine, and seek to mend;
That I may rise, and stand, o'erthrow me, and bend
Your force, to break, blow, burn, and make me new.
I, like an usurped town, to another due,
Labour to admit you, but O, to no end.
Reason, your viceroy in me, me should defend,
But is captived, and proves weak or untrue.
Yet dearly I love you, and would be loved fain,
But am betrothed unto your enemy;
Divorce me, untie, or break that knot again,
Take me to you, imprison me, for I
Except you enthrall me, never shall be free,
Nor ever chaste, except you ravish me.

GOOD FRIDAY, 1613
RIDING WESTWARD

LET man's soul be a sphere, and then, in this,
Th'intelligence that moves, devotion is;
And as the other spheres, by being grown
Subject to foreign motion, lose their own,
And being by others hurried every day,
Scarce in a year their natural form obey:
Pleasure or business, so, our souls admit
For their first mover, and are whirled by it.
Hence is't, that I am carried towards the west
This day, when my soul's form bends toward the east.
There I should see a sun by rising set,
And by that setting endless day beget;

But that Christ on His cross did rise and fall,
Sin had eternally benighted all.
Yet dare I almost be glad, I do not see
That spectacle of too much weight for me.
Who sees Gods face, that is self-life, must die;
What a death were it then to see God die?
It made His own lieutenant, Nature, shrink,
It made His footstool crack, and the sun wink.
Could I behold those hands, which span the poles,
And turn all spheres at once, pierced with those holes?
Could I behold that endless height, which is
Zenith to us and our antipodes,
Humbled below us? or that blood, which is
The seat of all our soul's, if not of His,
Made dirt of dust, or that flesh which was worn
By God for His apparel, ragg'd and torn?
If on these things I durst not look, durst I
On His distressed Mother cast mine eye,
Who was God's partner here, and furnished thus
Half of that sacrifice which ransomed us?
Though these things as I ride be from mine eye,
They're present yet unto my memory,
For that looks towards them;
                              and Thou look'st towards me,
O Saviour, as Thou hang'st upon the tree;
I turn my back to Thee but to receive
Corrections till Thy mercies bid Thee leave.
O think me worth Thine anger, punish me,
Burn off my rust, and my deformity;
Restore Thine image, so much, by Thy grace,
That Thou mayst know me, and I'll turn my face.

Twickenham Garden

Blasted with sighs, and surrounded with tears,
Hither I come to seek the spring,
And at mine eyes, and at mine ears,
   Receive such balms as else cure everything.
   But O! self-traitor, I do bring
The spider Love, which transubstantiates all,
And can convert manna to gall;
And that this place may thoroughly be thought
True paradise, I have the serpent brought.

'Twere wholesomer for me that winter did
   Benight the glory of this place,
And that a grave frost did forbid
   These trees to laugh and mock me to my face;
   But that I may not this disgrace
Endure, nor yet leave loving, Love, let me
Some senseless piece of this place be;
Make me a mandrake, so I may groan here,
Or a stone fountain weeping out my year.

Hither with crystal phials, lovers come,
   And take my tears, which are love's wine.
And try your mistress' tears at home,
   For all are false, that taste not just like mine.
   Alas! hearts do not in eyes shine,
Nor can you more judge woman's thoughts by tears,
Than by her shadow, what she wears.
O perverse sex, where none is true but she,
Who's therefore true, because her truth kills me.

Ben Jonson (1573–1637)

To Celia

Drink to me, only with thine eyes,
　　And I will pledge with mine;
Or leave a kiss but in the cup,
　　And I'll not look for wine.
The thirst, that from the soul doth rise,
　　Doth ask a drink divine:
But might I of Jove's nectar sup,
　　I would not change for thine.

I sent thee late a rosie wreath,
　　Not so much honoring thee,
As giving it a hope, that there
　　It could not withered be.
But thou thereon didst only breathe,
　　And sent'st it back to me:
Since when it grows, and smells, I swear,
　　Not of itself, but thee.

A Hymn to God the Father

Hear me, O God!
    A broken heart,
        Is my best part:
Use still thy rod,
        That I may prove
        Therein, thy Love.

If thou hadst not
        Been stern to me,
        But left me free,
I had forgot
        Myself and thee.

For sin's so sweet,
        As minds ill bent
        Rarely repent,
Until they meet
        Their punishment.

Who more can crave
        Than thou hast done,
        That gav'st a Son,
To free a slave?
        First made of nought;
        With All since bought.

Sin, Death, and Hell,
        His glorious Name
        Quite overcame,
Yet I rebel,
        And slight the same.

But, I'll come in,
    Before my loss,
    Me farther toss,
As sure to win
    Under his Cross.

THE HOUR-GLASS

CONSIDER this small dust, here in the glass,
    By atoms moved:
Could you believe that this the body was
    Of one that loved;
And in his mistress' flame playing like a fly,
Was turned to cinders by her eye:
Yes; and in death, as life unblest,
    To have't exprest,
Even ashes of lovers find no rest.

Edward, Lord Herbert of Cherbury (1583–1648)

To His Watch

WHEN HE COULD NOT SLEEP

UNCESSANT Minutes, whil'st you move you tell
The time that tells our life, which though it run
Never so fast or far, your new begun
Short steps shall overtake; for though life well

May scape his own account, it shall not yours,
You are Death's auditors, that both divide
And sum what ere that life inspired endures
Past a beginning, and through you we bide

The doom of Fate, whose unrecalled decree
You date, bring, execute; making what's new,
Ill and good, old, for as we die in you,
You die in Time, Time in Eternity.

Portrait of Edward Herbert, possibly after Isaac Oliver (c. 1604)

SONNET OF BLACK BEAUTY

BLACK beauty, which above that common light,
Whose Power can no colours here renew,
　But those which darkness can again subdue,
Do'st still remain unvaryed to the sight,
And like an object equal to the view,
　Art neither changed with day, nor hid with night;
　When all these colours which the world call bright,
And which old Poetry doth so persue,
Are with the night so perished and gone,
　That of their being there remains no mark,
Thou still abidest so intirely one,
　That we may know thy blackness is a spark
Of light inaccessible, and alone
　Our darkness which can make us think it dark.

IN A GLASS-WINDOW FOR INCONSTANCY

LOVE, of this clearest, frailest glass,
　Divide the properties, so as
In the division may appear
Clearness for me, frailty for her.

Aurelian Townshend (1583–1643)

Upon Kind and True Love

'Tis not how witty, nor how free,
Nor yet how beautiful she be,
But how much kind and true to me.
Freedom and Wit none can confine,
And Beauty like the Sun doth shine,
But kind and true are onely mine.

Let others with attention sit,
To listen, and admire her wit,
That is a rock where I'll not split.
Let others dote upon her eyes,
And burn their hearts for sacrifice,
Beauty's a calm where danger lies.

But Kind and True have been long tried
A harbour where we may confide,
And safely there at anchor ride.
From change of winds there we are free,
And need not fear storm's tyranny,
Nor pirate, though a prince he be.

Henry King (1592–1669)

SONNET

TELL me no more how fair she is,
  I have no mind to hear
The story of that distant bliss
  I never shall come near:
By sad experience I have found
That her perfection is my wound.

And tell me not how fond I am
  To tempt a daring Fate,
From whence no triumph ever came,
  But to repent too late:
There is some hope ere long I may
In silence dote myself away.

I ask no pity (Love) from thee,
  Nor will thy justice blame,
So that thou wilt not envy me
  The glory of my flame:
Which crowns my heart when ere it dyes,
In that it falls her sacrifice.

THE EXEQUY

A<small>CCEPT</small>, thou shrine of my dead saint,
Instead of dirges this complaint;
And for sweet flowers to crown thy hearse,
Receive a strew of weeping verse
From thy grieved friend, whom thou might'st see
Quite melted into tears for thee.

Dear loss! since thy untimely fate,
My task hath been to meditate
On thee, on thee! Thou art the book,
The library whereon I look,
Though almost blind. For thee, loved clay,
I languish out, not live, the day,
Using no other exercise
But what I practise with mine eyes:
By which wet glasses I find out
How lazily time creeps about
To one that mourns: this, only this
My exercise and business is:
So I compute the weary hours
With sighs dissolved into showers.

Nor wonder if my time go thus
Backward and most preposterous;
Thou hast benighted me; thy set
This eve of blackness did beget,
Who wast my day (though overcast
Before thou hadst thy noontide past):
And I remember must in tears,
Thou scarce hadst seen so many years
As day tells hours. By thy clear sun
My love and fortune first did run;
But thou wilt never more appear
Folded within my hemisphere,
Since both thy light and motion,
Like a fled star, is fall'n and gone,
And 'twixt me and my soul's dear wish
The earth now interposed is,
Which such a strange eclipse doth make
As ne'er was read in almanac.

I could allow thee for a time
To darken me and my sad clime;
Were it a month, a year, or ten,
I would thy exile live till then,
And all that space my mirth adjourn,
So thou wouldst promise to return,
And putting off thy ashy shroud
At length disperse this sorrow's cloud.

But woe is me! the longest date
Too narrow is to calculate
These empty hopes: never shall I
Be so much blest as to descry
A glimpse of thee, till that day come
Which shall the earth to cinders doom,
And a fierce fever must calcine
The body of this world like thine,
My little world! That fit of fire
Once off, our bodies shall aspire
To our souls' bliss: then we shall rise
And view ourselves with clearer eyes
In that calm region where no night
Can hide us from each other's sight.

Meantime, thou hast her, earth: much good
May my harm do thee! Since it stood
With Heavens will I might not call
Her longer mine, I give thee all
My short-lived right and interest
In her, whom living I loved best.
With a most free and bounteous grief,
I give thee what I could not keep.
Be kind to her, and prithee look
Thou write into thy Doomsday book
Each parcel of this rarity
Which in thy casket shrined doth lie,
See that thou make the reck'ning straight,
And yield her back again by weight;
For thou must audit on thy trust
Each grain and atom of this dust,
As thou wilt answer Him that lent,
Not gave, thee my dear monument.

So close the ground, and 'bout her shade
Black curtains draw: my bride is laid.

Sleep on, my Love, in thy cold bed
Never to be disquieted!
My last good-night! Thou wilt not wake
Till I thy fate shall overtake:
Till age, or grief, or sickness must
Marry my body to that dust
It so much loves; and fill the room
My heart keeps empty in thy tomb.
Stay for me there: I will not fail
To meet thee in that hollow vale.
And think not much of my delay:
I am already on the way,
And follow thee with all the speed
Desire can make, or sorrows breed.
Each minute is a short degree,
And every hour a step towards thee.
At night when I betake to rest,
Next morn I rise nearer my West
Of life, almost by eight hours sail,
Than when sleep breathed his drowsy gale.

Thus from the Sun my Bottom steers,
And my days Compass downward bears:
Nor labour I to stem the tide
Through which to Thee I swiftly glide.

'Tis true – with shame and grief I yield –
Thou, like the van, first took'st the field,
And gotten hast the victory
In thus adventuring to die
Before me, whose more years might crave
A just precedence in the grave.
But hark! my pulse, like a soft drum,
Beats my approach, tells thee I come;
And slow howe'er my marches be,
I shall at last sit down by thee.

The thought of this bids me go on,
And wait my dissolution
With hope and comfort. Dear – forgive
The crime – I am content to live
Divided, with but half a heart,
Till we shall meet and never part.

Mary Forbes, 'A Spray of Flowers' (1768)

A Contemplation Upon Flowers

Brave flowers – that I could gallant it like you,
   And be as little vain!
You come abroad, and make a harmless show,
   And to your beds of earth again.
You are not proud: you know your birth,
For your embroidered garments are from earth.

You do obey your months and times, but I
   Would have it ever Spring:
My fate would know no Winter, never die,
   Nor think of such a thing.
O that I could my bed of earth but view
And smile, and look as cheerfully as you!

O teach me to see Death and not to fear,
   But rather to take truce!
How often have I seen you at a bier,
   And there look fresh and spruce!
You fragrant flowers! then teach me, that my breath
Like yours may sweeten and perfume my death.

Francis Quarles (1592–1644)

WHEREFORE HIDEST THOU THY FACE?

Job 13:24

WHY dost thou shade thy lovely face? O why
Doth that eclipsing hand so long deny
The Sun-shine of thy soul-enliv'ning eye?

Without that Light, what light remains in me?
Thou art my Life, my Way, my Light; in thee
I live, I move, and by thy beams I see.

Thou art my Life; if thou but turn away,
My life's a thousand deaths: thou art my Way;
Without thee, Lord, I travel not, but stray.

My Light thou art; without thy glorious sight,
Mine eyes are darkened with perpetual night.
My God, thou art my Way, my Life, my Light.

Thou art my Way; I wander, if thou fly:
Thou art my Light; if hid, how blind am I!
Thou art my Life; if thou withdraw, I die.

Mine eyes are blind and dark; I cannot see;
To whom, or whither should my darkness flee,
But to the Light? And who's that Light but thee?

My path is lost; my wandering steps do stray;
I cannot safely go, nor safely stay;
Whom should I seek but thee, my Path, my Way?

O, I am dead: to whom shall I, poor I,
Repair? to whom shall my sad ashes fly
But Life? And where is Life but in thine eye?

And yet thou turn'st away thy face, and fly'st me;
And yet I sue for grace, and thou deny'st me;
Speak, art thou angry, Lord, or only try'st me?

Unscreen those Heav'nly lamps, or tell me why
Thou shad'st thy face; perhaps thou think'st, no eye
Can view those flames, and not drop down and die.

If that be all, shine forth, and draw thee nigher;
Let me behold and die, for my desire
Is Phoenix-like to perish in that fire.

Death-conquered Laz'rus was redeemed by thee;
If I am dead, Lord, set death's prisoner free;
Am I more spent, or stink I worse than he?

If my puffed light be out, give leave to tine
My flameless snuff at that bright Lamp of thine;
O what's thy Light the less for lighting mine?

If I have lost my Path, great Shepherd, say,
Shall I still wander in a doubtful way?
Lord, shall a Lamb of Israel's sheepfold stray?

Thou art the Pilgrim's Path; the blind man's Eye;
The dead man's Life; on thee my hopes rely;
If thou remove, I err; I grope; I die.

Disclose thy Sun beams; close thy wings, and stay;
See, see how I am blind, and dead, and stray,
O thou, that art my Light, my Life, my Way.

MY BELOVED IS MINE, AND I AM HIS

Canticles 2:16

E'EN like two little bank-dividing brooks,
That wash the pebbles with their wanton streams,
And having ranged and searched a thousand nooks,
   Meet both at length in silver-breasted Thames,
     Where in a greater current they conjoin:
So I my best-beloved's am; so he is mine.

Ev'n so we met; and after long pursuit,
   Ev'n so we joined; we both became entire;
No need for either to renew a suit,
   For I was flax and he was flames of fire:
     Our firm-united souls did more than twine;
So I my best-beloved's am; so he is mine.

If all those glitt'ring Monarchs that command
   The servile quarters of this earthly ball,
Should tender, in exchange, their shares of land,
   I would not change my fortunes for them all:
     Their wealth is but a counter to my coin:
The world's but theirs; but my beloved's mine.

Nay more; if the fair Thespian Ladies all
   Should heap together their diviner treasure:
That treasure should be deemed a price too small
   To buy a minutes lease of half my pleasure.
     'Tis not the sacred wealth of all the nine
Can buy my heart from him, or his, from being mine.

Nor Time, nor Place, nor Chance, nor Death can bow
   My least desires unto the least remove;
He's firmly mine by oath; I his by vow;
    He's mine by faith; and I am his by love;
      He's mine by water; I am his by wine;
Thus I my best-beloved's am; thus he is mine.

He is my Altar; I his Holy Place;
   I am his guest; and he, my living food;
I'm his by penitence; he mine by grace;
    I'm his by purchase; he is mine by blood;
      He's my supporting elm; and I his vine:
Thus I my best-beloved's am; thus he is mine.

He gives me wealth, I give him all my vows:
   I give him songs; he gives me length of days.
With wreaths of grace he crowns my conqu'ring brows:
    And I his Temples with a crown of Praise,
      Which he accepts as an ev'rlasting sign,
That I my best-beloved's am; that he is mine.

Joos van Cleve, 'The Last Judgment' (c. 1522)

THE AUTHOR'S DREAM

MY sins are like the hairs upon my head,
And raise their audit to as high a score.
In this they differ: these do daily shed;
But ah! my sins grow daily more and more.
    If by my hairs thou number out my sins,
    Heaven make me bald before the day begins.

My sins are like the sands upon the shore,
Which every ebb lays open to the eye.
In this they differ: these are covered o'er
With every tide; my sins still open lie.
    If thou wilt make my head a sea of tears,
    O they will hide the sins of all my years.

My sins are like the Stars within the skies,
In view, in number, even as bright as great.
In this they differ: these do set and rise;
But ah! my sins do rise, but never set.
    Shine Son of glory, and my sins are gone
    Like twinkling Stars before the rising Sun.

George Herbert (1593–1633)

EASTER

Rise, heart; thy Lord is risen. Sing his praise
    Without delays,
Who takes thee by the hand, that thou likewise
    With him mayst rise:
That, as his death calcined thee to dust,
His life may make thee gold, and much more just.

Awake, my lute, and struggle for thy part
    With all thy art.
The cross taught all wood to resound his name
    Who bore the same.
His stretched sinews taught all strings, what key
Is best to celebrate this most high day.

Consort both heart and lute, and twist a song
    Pleasant and long;
Or since all music is but three parts vied
    And multiplied;
O let thy blessed Spirit bear a part,
And make up our defects with his sweet art.

EASTER WINGS

L ORD, who createdst man in wealth and store,
Though foolishly he lost the same,
   Decaying more and more,
     Till he became
      Most poor:

      With Thee
     O let me rise
   As larks, harmoniously,
And sing this day Thy victories:
Then shall the fall further the flight in me.

My tender age in sorrow did begin:
   And still with sicknesses and shame
     Thou didst so punish sin,
      That I became
      Most thin.

      With Thee
     Let me combine,
   And feel this day Thy victory;
For, if I imp my wing on Thine,
Affliction shall advance the flight in me.

Marcantonio Bassetti, 'Portrait of an Old Man With a Book'

AFFLICTION

WHEN first Thou didst entice to Thee my heart,
    I thought the service brave:
So many joys I writ down for my part,
    Besides what I might have
Out of my stock of natural delights,
Augmented with Thy gracious benefits.

I lookèd on Thy furniture so fine,
    And made it fine to me;
Thy glorious household stuff did me entwine,
    And 'tice me unto Thee.
Such stars I counted mine: both heaven and earth
Paid me my wages in a world of mirth.

What pleasures could I want, whose King I served,
    Where joys my fellows were?
Thus argued into hopes, my thoughts reserved
    No place for grief or fear;
Therefore my sudden soul caught at the place,
And made her youth and fierceness seek Thy face.

At first thou gavest me milk and sweetness;
    I had my wish and way.
My days were strewed with flowers and happiness;
    There was no month but May.
But with my years sorrow did twist and grow,
And made a party unawares for woe.

My flesh began unto my soul in pain,
   Sicknesses clave my bones,
Consuming agues dwell in every vein,
   And tune my breath to groans;
Sorrow was all my soul; I scarce believed,
Till grief did tell me roundly, that I lived.

When I got health, Thou took'st away my life —
   And more; for my friends die.
My mirth and edge was lost: a blunted knife
   Was of more use than I.
Thus, thin and lean, without a fence or friend,
I was blown through with every storm and wind.

Whereas my birth and spirit rather took
   The way that takes the town,
Thou didst betray me to a lingering book,
   And wrap me in a gown.
I was entangled in the world of strife,
Before I had the power to change my life.

Yet, for I threatened oft the siege to raise,
   Not simpering all mine age,
Thou often didst with academic praise
   Melt and dissolve my rage.
I took thy sweetened pill, till I came near;
I could not go away, nor persevere.

Yet, lest perchance I should too happy be
   In my unhappiness,
Turning my purge to food, Thou throwest me
   Into more sicknesses.
Thus doth Thy power cross-bias me, not making
Thine own gift good, yet me from my ways taking.

Now I am here, what thou wilt do with me
   None of my books will show.
I read, and sigh, and wish I were a tree –
   For sure, then, I should grow
To fruit or shade; at least some bird would trust
Her household to me, and I should be just.

Yet, though Thou troublest me, I must be meek;
   In weakness must be stout:
Well, I will change the service, and go seek
   Some other master out.
Ah, my dear God! though I am clean forgot,
Let me not love Thee, if I love Thee not.

JORDAN (1)

WHO says that fictions only and false hair
   Become a verse? Is there in truth no beauty?
Is all good structure in a winding stair?
May no lines pass, except they do their duty
   Not to a true, but painted chair?

Is it not verse, except enchanted groves
And sudden arbours shadow course-spun lines?
Must purling streams refresh a lovers loves?
Must all be vail'd, while he that reads, divines,
   Catching the sense at two removes?

Shepherds are honest people; let them sing:
Riddle who list, for me, and pull for prime,
I envy no man's nightingale or spring;
Nor let them punish me with loss of rhyme,
   Who plainly say, My God, My King.

THE TEMPER

How should I praise thee, Lord!
                    how should my rhymes
  Gladly engrave thy love in steel,
  If what my soul doth feel sometimes,
    My soul might ever feel!

Although there were some forty heav'ns, or more,
  Sometimes I peer above them all;
  Sometimes I hardly reach a score,
    Sometimes to hell I fall.

O rack me not to such a vast extent;
  Those distances belong to thee:
  The world's too little for thy tent,
    A grave too big for me.

Wilt thou meet arms with man, that thou dost stretch
  A crumb of dust from heav'n to hell?
  Will great God measure with a wretch?
    Shall he thy stature spell?

O let me, when thy roof my soul hath hid,
  O let me roost and nestle there:
  Then of a sinner thou art rid,
    And I of hope and fear.

Yet take thy way; for sure thy way is best:
  Stretch or contract me thy poor debter:
  This is but tuning of my breast,
    To make the music better.

Whether I fly with angels, fall with dust,
    Thy hands made both, and I am there.
    Thy power and love, my love and trust,
        Make one place everywhere.

VIRTUE

SWEET day, so cool, so calm, so bright,
    The bridal of the earth and sky:
The dew shall weep thy fall tonight;
        For thou must die.

Sweet rose, whose hue angrie and brave
Bids the rash gazer wipe his eye,
Thy root is ever in its grave,
        And thou must die.

Sweet spring, full of sweet dayes and roses,
A box where sweets compacted lie,
My musick shows ye have your closes,
        And all must die.

Onely a sweet and vertuous soul,
Like seasoned timber, never gives;
But though the whole world turn to coal,
        Then chiefly lives.

DISCIPLINE

THROW away thy rod,
   Throw away thy wrath:
   O my God,
Take the gentle path.

For my heart's desire
Unto thine is bent:
   I aspire
To a full consent.

Nor a word or look
I affect to own,
   But by book,
And thy book alone.

Though I fail, I weep;
Though I halt in pace,
   Yet I creep
To the throne of grace.

Then let wrath remove;
Love will do the deed:
   For with love
Stony hearts will bleed.

Love is swift of foot;
Love's a man of war,
   And can shoot,
And can hit from far.

Who can scape his bow?
That which wrought on thee,
   Brought thee low,
Needs must work on me.

Throw away thy rod;
Though man frailties hath,
   Thou art God:
Throw away thy wrath.

THE PEARL

Matthew 13

I KNOW the ways of learning; both the head
And pipes that feed the press, and make it run;
What reason hath from nature borrowed,
Or of itself, like a good housewife, spun
In laws and policy; what the stars conspire,
What willing nature speaks, what forced by fire;
Both th'old discoveries, and the new-found seas,
The stock and surplus, cause and history:
All these stand open, or I have the keys:
   Yet I love thee.

I know the ways of honour, what maintains
The quick returns of courtesy and wit:
In vies of favours whether party gains,
When glory swells the heart, and moldeth it
To all expressions both of hand and eye,
Which on the world a true love-knot may tie,
And bear the bundle, wheresoe'er it goes:
How many drams of spirit there must be
To sell my life unto my friends or foes:
    Yet I love thee.

I know the ways of pleasure, the sweet strains,
The lullings and the relishes of it;
The propositions of hot blood and brains;
What mirth and music mean; what love and wit
Have done these twenty hundred years, and more:
I know the projects of unbridled store:
My stuff is flesh, not brass; my senses live,
And grumble oft, that they have more in me
Then he that curbs them, being but one to five:
    Yet I love thee.

I know all these, and have them in my hand:
Therefore not sealed, but with open eyes
I fly to thee, and fully understand
Both the main sale, and the commodities;
And at what rate and price I have thy love,
With all the circumstances that may move:
Yet through these labyrinths, not my groveling wit,
But thy silk twist let down from heav'n to me,
Did both conduct and teach me, how by it
    To climb to thee.

THE CHURCH-FLOOR

MARK you the floor? That square and speckled stone,
　　Which looks so firm and strong,
　　　　Is *Patience*:

And th'other black and grave, wherewith each one
　　Is checkered all along,
　　　　Humility:

The gentle rising, which on either hand
　　Leads to the Quire above,
　　　　Is *Confidence*:

But the sweet cement, which in one sure band
　　Ties the whole frame, is Love
　　　　And *Charity*.

　　Hither sometimes Sin steals, and stains
　　The marbles neat and curious veins:
But all is cleansed when the marble weeps.
　　Sometimes Death, puffing at the door,
　　Blows all the dust about the floore:
But while he thinks to spoil the room, he sweeps.
　　Blest be the Architect, whose art
　　Could build so strong in a weak heart.

LIFE

I MADE a posy while the day ran by:
Here will I smell my remnant out, and tie
   My life within this band.
But Time did beckon to the flowers, and they
By noon most cunningly did steal away,
   And withered in my hand.

My hand was next to them, and then my heart;
I took, without more thinking, in good part
   Time's gentle admonition;
Who did so sweetly death's sad taste convey,
Making my mind to smell my fatal day,
   Yet sugring the suspicion.

Farewell, dear flowers, sweetly your time ye spent,
Fit, while ye lived, for smell or ornament,
   And after death for cures.
I follow straight without complaints or grief,
Since if my scent be good, I care not, if
   It be as short as yours.

Jan Brueghel the Elder, 'Still Life With Flowers in a Glass'

THE COLLAR

I STRUCK the board, and cryed, No more;
     I will abroad.
  What? shall I ever sigh and pine?
My lines and life are free; free as the rode,
    Loose as the wind, as large as store.
        Shall I be still in suit?
    Have I no harvest but a thorn
    To let me blood, and not restore
What I have lost with cordial fruit?
        Sure there was wine,
    Before my sighs did dry it: there was corn
      Before my tears did drown it.
    Is the year only lost to me?
      Have I no bays to crown it?
No flowers, no garlands gay? all blasted?
       All wasted?
    Not so, my heart: but there is fruit,
        And thou hast hands.
     Recover all thy sigh-blown age
On double pleasures: leave thy cold dispute
Of what is fit and not; forsake thy cage,
       Thy rope of sands,
Which petty thoughts have made, and made to thee
    Good cable, to enforce and draw,
       And be thy law,
    While thou didst wink and wouldst not see.
       Away! take heed:
       I will abroad.

Call in thy deaths head there: tie up thy fears.
  He that forbears
   To suit and serve his need,
    Deserves his load.
But as I raved and grew more fierce and wild,
   At every word,
  Methought I heard one calling, *Childe*:
    And I replied, *My Lord*.

REDEMPTION

HAVING been tenant long to a rich Lord,
  Not thriving, I resolved to be bold,
  And make a suit unto him, to afford
A new small-rented lease, and cancel th'old.

In heaven at his manor I him sought:
  They told me there, that he was lately gone
  About some land, which he had dearly bought
Long since on earth, to take possession.

I straight returned, and knowing his great birth,
  Sought him accordingly in great resorts –
  In cities, theatres, gardens, parks, and courts:
At length I heard a ragged noise and mirth

  Of thieves and murderers: there I him espied,
Who straight, *Your suit is granted*, said, and died.

THE ELIXIR

Teach me, my God and King,
  In all things Thee to see,
And what I do in anything,
To do it as for Thee.

Not rudely, as a beast,
To run into action;
But still to make Thee prepossest,
And give it his perfection.

A man that looks on glass,
On it may stay his eye,
Or, if he pleaseth, through it pass,
And then the heav'n espy.

All may of Thee partake;
Nothing can be so mean
Which with his tincture (for Thy sake)
Will not grow bright and clean.

A servant with this clause
Makes drudgery divine:
Who sweeps a room as for Thy laws,
Makes that and th'action fine.

This is the famous stone
That turneth all to gold;
For that which God doth touch and own
Cannot for less be told.

LOVE

Love bade me welcome, yet my soul drew back,
 Guilty of dust and sin.
But quick-eyed Love, observing me grow slack
 From my first entrance in,
Drew nearer to me, sweetly questioning
 If I lacked anything.

'A guest,' I answered, 'worthy to be here';
 Love said, 'You shall be he.'
'I, the unkind, the ungrateful? Ah my dear,
 I cannot look on thee.'
Love took my hand and smiling did reply,
 'Who made the eyes but I?'

'Truth, Lord, but I have marred them; let my shame
 Go where it doth deserve.'
'And know you not,' says Love, 'who bore the blame?'
 'My dear, then I will serve.'
'You must sit down,' says Love, 'and taste my meat.'
 So I did sit and eat.

Thomas Carew (1595–1639)

TO MY INCONSTANT MISTRESS

WHEN thou, poor excommunicate
  From all the joys of love, shalt see
The full reward and glorious fate
  Which my strong faith shall purchase me,
  Then curse thine own inconstancy.

A fairer hand than thine shall cure
  That heart, which thy false oaths did wound;
And to my soul a soul more pure
  Than thine shall by Love's hand be bound,
  And both with equal glory crowned.

Then shalt thou weep, entreat, complain
  To Love, as I did once to thee;
When all thy tears shall be as vain
  As mine were then, for thou shalt be
  Damned for thy false apostasy.

Veronese, 'The Allegory of Love: Unfaithfulness' (1570)

MEDIOCRITY IN LOVE REJECTED

GIVE me more love or more disdain;
   The torrid or the frozen zone
Bring equal ease unto my pain,
   The temperate affords me none:
Either extreme of love or hate,
Is sweeter than a calm estate.

Give me a storm; if it be love,
   Like Danaë in that golden shower,
I swim in pleasure; if it prove
   Disdain, that torrent will devour
My vulture-hopes; and he's possessed
Of heaven, that's but from hell released.
      Then crown my joys or cure my pain:
      Give me more love or more disdain.

ETERNITY OF LOVE PROTESTED

How ill doth he deserve a lover's name
   Whose pale weak flame
    Cannot retain
His heat, in spite of absence or disdain;
But doth at once, like paper set on fire
   Burn and expire!
True love can never change his seat,
Nor did he ever love that could retreat.

That noble flame, which my breast keeps alive,
    Shall still survive
    When my soul's fled;
Nor shall my love die, when my body's dead;
That shall wait on me to the lower shade,
    And never fade:
My very ashes in their urn
Shall, like a hallowed lamp, for ever burn.

AN ELEGY

UPON THE DEATH OF THE DEAN OF
ST PAULS, DR JOHN DONNE

CAN we not force from widowed poetry,
  Now thou art dead, great Donne, one elegy,
To crown thy hearse? Why yet dare we not trust,
Though with unkneaded dough-baked prose, thy dust,
Such as the unscissored lecturer, from the flower
Of fading rhetoric, short-lived as his hour,
Dry as the sand that measures it, might lay
Upon the ashes on the funeral day?
Have we no tune nor voice? Didst thou dispense
Through all our language both the words and sense?
'Tis a sad truth. The pulpit may her plain
And sober Christian precepts still retain;
Doctrines it may, and wholesome uses, frame,
Grave homilies and lectures; but the flame
Of thy brave soul, that shot such heat and light,
As burned our earth, and made our darkness bright,
Committed holy rapes upon our will,
Did through the eye the melting heart distil,
And the deep knowledge of dark truths so teach,
As sense might judge what fancy could not reach,
Must be desired for ever. So the fire,
That fills with spirit and heat the Delphic choir,
Which, kindled first by thy Promethean breath,
Glowed here awhile, lies quenched now in thy death.
The Muses' garden, with pedantic weeds
O'erspread, was purged by thee; the lazy seeds
Of servile imitation thrown away,
And fresh invention planted; thou didst pay

The debts of our penurious bankrupt age;
Licentious thefts, that make poetic rage
A mimic fury, when our souls must be
Possessed, or with Anacreon's ecstacy,
Or Pindar's, not their own; the subtle cheat
Of sly exchanges, and the juggling feat
Of two-edged words, or whatsoever wrong
By ours was done the Greek or Latin tongue,
Thou hast redeemed, and opened us a mine
Of rich and pregnant fancy; drawn a line
Of masculine expression, which, had good
Old Orpheus seen, or all the ancient brood
Our superstitious fools admire, and hold
Their lead more precious than thy burnished gold,
Thou hadst been their exchequer, and no more
They each in other's dust had searched for ore.
Thou shalt yield no precedence, but of time,
And the blind fate of language, whose tuned chime
More charms the outward sense: yet thou mayst claim
From so great disadvantage greater fame,
Since to the awe of thy imperious wit
Our troublesome language bends, made only fit
With her tough thick-ribbed hoops to gird about
Thy giant fancy, which had proved too stout
For their soft melting phrases. As in time
They had the start, so did they cull the prime
Buds of invention many a hundred year,
And left the rifled fields, besides the fear
To touch their harvest; yet from those bare lands,
Of what is only thine, thy only hands
(And that their smallest work) have gleaned more
Than all those times and tongues could reap before.

But thou art gone, and thy strict laws will be
Too hard for libertines in poetry;
They will recall the goodly exiled train
Of gods and goddesses, which in thy just reign
Were banished nobler poems; now with these,
The silenced tales o'th'Metamorphoses,
Shall stuff their lines, and swell the windy page,
Till verse, refined by thee in this last age,
Turn ballad-rhyme, or those old idols be
Adored again with new apostacy.
    O pardon me, that break with untuned verse
The reverend silence that attends thy hearse,
Whose solemn awful murmurs were to thee,
More than these rude lines, a loud elegy,
That did proclaim in a dumb eloquence
The death of all the arts: whose influence,
Grown feeble, in these panting numbers lies,
Gasping short-winded accents, and so dies.
So doth the swiftly-turning wheel not stand
In th'instant we withdraw the moving hand,
But some short time retain a faint weak course,
By virtue of the first impulsive force:
And so, whilst I cast on thy funeral pile
Thy crown of bays, oh let it crack awhile,
And spit disdain, till the devouring flashes
Suck all the moisture up, then turn to ashes.
    I will not draw thee envy to engross
All thy perfections, or weep all our loss;
Those are too numerous for an elegy,
And this too great to be expressed by me,

Though every pen should share a distinct part.
Yet art thou theme enough to tire all art;
Let others carve the rest; it shall suffice
I on thy grave this epitaph incise:

> *Here lies a king that ruled, as he thought fit,*
> *The universal monarchy of wit;*
> *Here lie two flamens, and both those the best:*
> *Apollo's first, at last the true God's priest.*

GOOD COUNSEL TO A YOUNG MAID

GAZE not on thy beauty's pride,
Tender maid, in the false tide
That from lovers' eyes doth slide.

Let thy faithful crystal show
How thy colours come and go:
Beauty takes a foil from woe.

Love, that in those smooth streams lies
Under pity's fair disguise,
Will thy melting heart surprise.

Nets of passion's finest thread,
Snaring poems, will be spread,
All to catch thy maidenhead.

Then beware! for those that cure
Love's disease, themselves endure
For reward a calenture.

Rather let the lover pine,
Than his pale cheek should assign
A perpetual blush to thine.

Gerrit Van Honthorst, 'Young Woman Playing Viola da Gamba'

To a Lady, That Desired I Love Her

Now you have freely given me leave to love,
    What will you do?
Shall I your mirth or passion move
    When I begin to woo?
Will you torment, or scorn, or love me too?

Each petty beauty can disdain, and I,
    Spite of your hate,
Without your leave can see, and die.
    Dispense a nobler fate!
'Tis easy to destroy: you may create.

Then give me leave to love, and love me too:
    Not with design
To raise, as Love's curst rebels do,
    When puling poets whine,
Fame to their beauty, from their blubbered eyne.

Grief is a puddle, and reflects not clear
    Your beauty's rays;
Joys are pure streams; your eyes appear
    Sullen in sadder lays;
In chearful numbers they shine bright with praise,

Which shall not mention, to express you fair,
    Wounds, flames, and darts,
Storms in your brow, nets in your hair,
    Suborning all your parts,
Or to betray, or torture captive hearts.

I'll make your eyes like morning suns appear,
 As mild and fair;
Your brow as crystal smooth and clear;
 And your dishevelled hair
Shall flow like a calm region of the air.

Rich Nature's store, which is the poet's treasure,
 I'll spend to dress
Your beauties, if your mine of pleasure
 In equal thankfulness
You but unlock, so we each other bless.

To My Worthy Friend
Master George Sandys

ON HIS TRANSLATION OF THE PSALMS

I PRESS not to the choir, nor dare I greet
The holy place with my unhallowed feet;
My unwashed Muse pollutes not things divine
Nor mingles her prophaner notes with thine;
Here humbly, at the porch she stays,
And with glad ears sucks in thy sacred lays.
So devout penitents of old were wont,
Some without doore and some beneath the font,
To stand and hear the Church's liturgies,
Yet not assist the solemn exercise.
Sufficeth her, that she a lay-place gain,
To trim thy vestments, or but bear thy train;
Though nor in tune, nor wing she reach thy lark,
Her lyric feet may dance before the Ark.
Who knows, but that her wand'ring eyes, that run
Now hunting glow-worms, may adore the sun?

A pure flame may, shot by Almighty power
Into her breast, the earthy flame devour?
My eyes in penitential dew may steep
That brine, which they for sensual love did weep.
So, though'gainst Nature's course, fire may be quenched
With fire, and water be with water drenched,
Perhaps my restless soul, tired with pursuit
Of mortal beauty, seeking without fruit
Contentment there, which hath not, when enjoyed
Quenched all her thirst, nor satisfied, though cloyed,
Weary of her vain search below, above
In the first fair may find th'immortal love.
Prompted by thy example then, no more
In moulds of clay will I my God adore;
But tear those idols from my heart, and write
What his blest Spirit, not fond love, shall indite.
Then I no more shall court the verdant bay,
But the dry leafless trunk on Golgotha,
And rather strive to gain from thence one thorn,
Than all the flourishing wreaths by Laureates worn.

Sir William Davenant (1605—1668)

MORNING

THE lark now leaves his watry nest
    And climbing, shakes his dewy wings;
He takes this window for the east;
    And to implore your light, he sings,
Awake, awake, the morn will never rise,
Till she can dress her beauty at your eyes.

The merchant bows unto the seaman's star,
    The ploughman from the sun his seasons takes;
But still the lover wonders what they are,
    Who look for day before his mistress wakes.
Awake, awake, break through your veil of lawn!
Then draw your curtains, and begin the dawn.

Edward Frederick Brewtnall, 'Sleeping Beauty'

Edmund Waller (1606–1687)

THE SELF BANISHED

IT is not that I love you less
Than when before your feet I lay,
But to prevent the sad increase
Of hopeless love, I keep away.

In vain (alas!) for everything
Which I have known belong to you,
Your form does to my fancy bring,
And makes my old wounds bleed anew.

Who in the spring from the new sun
Already has a fever got,
Too late begins those shafts to shun,
Which Phœbus through his veins has shot.

Too late he would the pain assuage,
And to thick shadows does retire;
About with him he bears the rage,
And in his tainted blood the fire.

But vowed I have, and never must
Your banished servant trouble you;
For if I break, you may distrust
The vow I made to love you, too.

ON MY LADY ISABELLA
PLAYING ON THE LUTE

SUCH moving sounds, from such a careless touch,
So unconcerned herself, and we so much!
What art is this, that with so little pains
Transports us thus, and o'er our spirits reigns!
The trembling strings about her fingers crowd,
And tell their joy for every kiss aloud:
Small force there needs to make them tremble so;
Touched by that hand who would not tremble too?
Here Love takes stand, and while she charms the ear,
Empties his quiver on the listening deer;
Music so softens and disarms the mind,
That not an arrow does resistance find.
Thus the fair tyrant celebrates the prize,
And acts herself the triumph of her eyes.
So Nero once, with harp in hand, surveyed
His flaming Rome, and as it burnt he played.

John Milton (1608–1674)

ON SHAKESPEARE

WHAT needs my Shakespeare
                    for his honoured bones,
The labour of an age in piled stones,
Or that his hallowed relics should be hid
Under a star-ypointing pyramid?
Dear son of memory, great heir of fame,
What need'st thou such weak witness of thy name?
Thou in our wonder and astonishment
Hast built thyself a live-long monument.
For whilst to th'shame of slow-endeavouring art,
Thy easy numbers flow, and that each heart
Hath from the leaves of thy unvalued book,
Those Delphic lines with deep impression took,
Then thou our fancy of it self bereaving,
Dost make us marble with too much conceiving;
And so sepulchered in such pomp dost lie,
That kings for such a tomb would wish to die.

WHEN I CONSIDER HOW
MY LIGHT IS SPENT

SONNET 19

WHEN I consider how my light is spent
  Ere half my days in this dark world and wide,
And that one talent which is death to hide
Lodged with me useless, though my soul more bent
To serve therewith my Maker, and present
My true account, lest he returning chide,
'Doth God exact day-labour, light denied?'
I fondly ask. But Patience, to prevent
That murmur, soon replies: 'God doth not need
Either man's work or his own gifts: who best
Bear his mild yoke, they serve him best. His state
Is kingly; thousands at his bidding speed
And post o'er land and ocean without rest:
They also serve who only stand and wait.'

John Suckling (1609–1642)

SONG

WHY so pale and wan, fond lover?
   Prithee, why so pale?
Will, when looking well can't move her,
   Looking ill prevail?
   Prithee, why so pale?

Why so dull and mute, young sinner?
   Prithee, why so mute?
Will, when speaking well can't win her,
   Saying nothing do't?
   Prithee, why so mute?

Quit, quit, for shame, this will not move:
   This cannot take her.
If of herself she will not love,
   Nothing can make her:
   The devil take her!

O! FOR SOME HONEST LOVER'S GHOST

O! for some honest lover's ghost,
   Some kind unbodied post
Sent from the shades below!
I strangely long to know,
Whether the noble chaplets wear,
Those that their mistress' scorn did bear,
   Or those that were used kindly.

For whatsoe'er they tell us here
    To make those sufferings dear,
    'Twill there I fear be found,
    That to the being crowned
T'have loved alone will not suffice,
Unless we also have been wise,
    And have our loves enjoyed.

What posture can we think him in,
    That here unloved again
    Departs, and's thither gone
    Where each sits by his own?
Or how can that Elysium be
Where I my mistress still must see
    Circled in others' arms?

For there the judges all are just,
    And Sophonisba must
    Be his whom she held dear,
    Not his who loved her here:
The sweet Philoclea, since she died,
Lies by her Pirocles his side,
    Not by Amphialus.

Some bays, perchance, or myrtle bough,
    For difference crowns the brow
    Of those kind souls that were
    The noble martyrs here;
And if that be the only odds
(As who can tell?) ye kinder gods,
    Give me the woman here.

Richard Crashaw (1612–1649)

AN EPITAPH UPON HUSBAND AND WIFE
WHO DIED TOGETHER AND WERE BURIED TOGETHER

To these whom death again did wed,
  This grave's the second marriage-bed.
For though the hand of Fate could force
'Twixt soul and body a divorce,
It could not sever man and wife,
Because they both lived but one life.
Peace, good reader, do not weep;
Peace, the lovers are asleep.
They, sweet turtles, folded lie
In the last knot that love could tie.
And though they lie as they were dead,
Their pillow stone, their sheetes of lead
(Pillow hard, and sheets not warm)
Love made the bed; they'll take no harm.
Let them sleep, let them sleep on,
Till the stormy night be gone,
And the eternal morrow dawn;
Then the curtains will be drawn,
And they wake into a light
Whose day shall never die in night.

Abraham Cowley (1618–1667)

DRINKING

THE thirsty earth soaks up the rain,
    And drinks and gapes for drink again;
The plants suck in the earth, and are
With constant drinking fresh and fair;
The sea itself (which one would think
Should have but little need of drink)
Drinks twice ten thousand rivers up,
So filled that they o'erflow the cup.
The busy Sun (and one would guess
By's drunken fiery face no less)
Drinks up the sea, and when he's done,
The Moon and Stars drink up the Sun:
They drink and dance by their own light,
They drink and revel all the night:
Nothing in Nature's sober found,
But an eternal health goes round.
Fill up the bowl, then, fill it high,
Fill all the glasses there, for why
Should every creature drink but I?
Why, man of morals, tell me why?

Richard Lovelace (1618–1657)

To Lucasta, Going to the Wars

TELL me not (Sweet) I am unkind,
    That from the nunnery
Of thy chaste breast, and quiet mind,
    To war and arms I fly.

True; a new mistress now I chase,
    The first foe in the field;
And with a stronger faith embrace
    A sword, a horse, a shield.

Yet this inconstancy is such,
    As you too shall adore;
I could not love thee (Dear) so much,
    Loved I not honour more.

Andrew Marvell (1621–1678)

Bermudas

WHERE the remote Bermudas ride,
    In the ocean's bosom unespied,
From a small boat, that rowed along,
The listening winds received this song:

'What should we do but sing His praise
That led us through the watery maze,
Unto an isle so long unknown,
And yet far kinder than our own?
Where He the huge sea-monsters wracks,
That lift the deep upon their backs;
He lands us on a grassy stage,
Safe from the storms, and prelate's rage.
He gave us this eternal spring,
Which here enamels every thing,
And sends the fowls to us in care,
On daily visits through the air;
He hangs in shades the orange bright,
Like golden lamps in a green night,
And does in the pomegranates close
Jewels more rich than Ormus shows;
He makes the figs our mouths to meet,
And throws the melons at our feet;
But apples plants of such a price,
No tree could ever bear them twice;
With cedars chosen by His hand,
From Lebanon, He stores the land,
And makes the hollow seas, that roar,
Proclaim the ambergris on shore;
He cast (of which we rather boast)
The Gospel's pearl upon our coast,
And in these rocks for us did frame
A temple where to sound His name.
Oh! let our voice His praise exalt,
Till it arrive at Heaven's vault,
Which, thence (perhaps) rebounding, may
Echo beyond the Mexique Bay.'

Thus sung they, in the English boat,
An holy and a cheerful note;
And all the way, to guide their chime,
With falling oars they kept the time.

TO HIS COY MISTRESS

HAD we but world enough, and time,
This coyness, lady, were no crime.
We would sit down and think which way
To walk, and pass our long love's day;
Thou by the Indian Ganges' side
Shouldst rubies find; I by the tide
Of Humber would complain. I would
Love you ten years before the Flood;
And you should, if you please, refuse
Till the conversion of the Jews.
My vegetable love should grow
Vaster than empires, and more slow.
An hundred years should go to praise
Thine eyes, and on thy forehead gaze;
Two hundred to adore each breast,
But thirty thousand to the rest;
An age at least to every part,
And the last age should show your heart.
For, lady, you deserve this state,
Nor would I love at lower rate.

But at my back I always hear
Time's winged chariot hurrying near;
And yonder all before us lie
Deserts of vast eternity.
Thy beauty shall no more be found,
Nor, in thy marble vault, shall sound
My echoing song; then worms shall try
That long preserved virginity,
And your quaint honour turn to dust,
And into ashes all my lust.
The grave's a fine and private place,
But none I think do there embrace.

Now therefore, while the youthful hue
Sits on thy skin like morning dew,
And while thy willing soul transpires
At every pore with instant fires,
Now let us sport us while we may;
And now, like am'rous birds of prey,
Rather at once our time devour,
Than languish in his slow-chapped power.
Let us roll all our strength, and all
Our sweetness, up into one ball;
And tear our pleasures with rough strife
Thorough the iron gates of life.
Thus, though we cannot make our sun
Stand still, yet we will make him run.

Henry Vaughan (1621–1695)

THE SHOWER

'TWAS so; I saw thy birth. That drowsy lake
      From her faint bosom breathed thee, the disease
Of her sick waters and infectious ease.
      But now at even,
      Too gross for heaven,
Thou fall'st in tears, and weep'st for thy mistake.

Ah! it is so with me: oft have I pressed
      Heaven with a lazy breath; but fruitless this
      Pierced not; love only can with quick access
            Unlock the way,
            When all else stray,
The smoke and exhalations of the breast.

Yet, if as thou dost melt, and with thy train
      Of drops make soft the Earth, my eyes could weep
      O'er my hard heart, that's bound up and asleep;
            Perhaps at last,
            Some such showers past,
My God would give a sunshine after rain.

THE DWELLING-PLACE

WHAT happy, secret fountain,
    Fair shade or mountain,
Whose undiscovered virgin glory
Boasts it this day, though not in story,
Was then thy dwelling? Did some cloud,
Fixed to a tent, descend and shroud
My distressed Lord? Or did a star
Beckoned by thee, though high and far,
In sparkling smiles haste gladly down
To lodge light, and increase her own?
My dear, dear God! I do not know
What lodged thee then, nor where, nor how;
But I am sure, thou dost now come
Oft to a narrow, homely room,
Where thou too hast, but the least part,
My God, I mean my sinful heart.

Thomas Traherne (1638–1674)

NEWS

NEWS from a foreign country came,
   As if my treasures and my joys lay there;
So much it did my heart inflame,
'Twas wont to call my soul into mine ear;
     Which thither went to meet
     Th'approaching sweet,
  And on the threshold stood
  To entertain the secret good;
     It hovered there
    As if 'twould leave mine ear,
  And was so eager to embrace
The joyful tidings as they came,
That it could change its dwelling place
  To meet the voice of fame.

  As if new tidings were the things
Which did comprise my wished unknown treasure,
  Or else did bear them on their wings,
With so much joy they came, with so much pleasure,
     My soul stood at the gate
     To recreate
  Itself with bliss, and woo
  Its speedier approach; a fuller view
     It fain would take,
    Yet journeys back would make
  Unto my heart, as if'twould fain
Go out to meet, yet stay within,
Fitting a place to entertain
  And bring the tidings in.

What sacred instinct did inspire
My soul in childhood with an hope so strong?
   What secret force moved my desire
T'expect my joys beyond the seas, so young?
     Felicity I knew
     Was out of view;
  And being left alone,
  I thought all happiness was gone
    From earth; for this
   I longed for absent bliss,
 Deeming that sure beyond the seas,
Or else in something near at hand
Which I knew not, since nought did please
 I knew, my bliss did stand.

  But little did the infant dream
That all the treasures of the world were by,
   And that himself was so the cream
And crown of all which round about did lie.
    Yet thus it was! The gem,
    The diadem,
  The ring enclosing all
  That stood upon this earthen ball;
    The heav'nly eye,
   Much wider than the sky,
 Wherein they all included were;
The love, the soul, that was the king
Made to possess them, did appear
 A small and little thing.

John Wilmot, Earl of Rochester (1647–1680)

UPON NOTHING

NOTHING, thou elder brother even to shade,
    That hadst a being ere the world was made,
And (well fixed) art alone of ending not afraid.
Ere time and place were, time and place were not,
When primitive Nothing Something straight begot,
Then all proceeded from the great united – What?
Something, the general attribute of all,
Severed from thee, its sole original,
Into thy boundless self must undistinguished fall.
Yet Something did thy mighty power command,
And from thy fruitful emptiness's hand,
Snatched men, beasts, birds, fire, water, air, and land.
Matter, the wickedest offspring of thy race,
By Form assisted, flew from thy embrace,
And rebel Light obscured thy reverend dusky face.
With Form and Matter, Time and Place did join,
Body, thy foe, with these did leagues combine
To spoil thy peaceful realm, and ruin all thy line.
But turncoat Time assists the foe in vain,
And, bribed by thee, assists thy short-lived reign,
And to thy hungry womb drives back thy slaves again.
Though mysteries are barred from laic eyes,
And the Divine alone with warrant pries
Into thy bosom, where thy truth in private lies,
Yet this of thee the wise may freely say,
Thou from the virtuous nothing takest away,
And to be part of thee the wicked wisely pray.

Great Negative, how vainly would the wise
Inquire, define, distinguish, teach, devise?
Didst thou not stand to point their dull philosophies?
Is, or is not, the two great ends of Fate,
And true or false, the subject of debate,
That perfects, or destroys, the vast designs of State,
When they have racked the politician's breast,
Within thy bosom most securely rest,
And, when reduced to thee, are least unsafe and best.
But Nothing, why does Something still permit
That sacred monarchs should at council sit
With persons highly thought at best for nothing fit?
While weighty Something modestly abstains
From princes' coffers, and from statesmen's brains,
And Nothing there like stately Nothing reigns,
Nothing, who dwellest with fools in grave disguise,
For whom they reverend shapes and forms devise,
Lawn sleeves, and furs, and gowns,
                          when they like thee look wise.
French truth, Dutch prowess, British policy,
Hibernian learning, Scotch civility,
Spaniard's dispatch, Dane's wit are mainly seen in thee.
The great man's gratitude to his best friend,
King's promises, whore's vows, towards thee they bend,
Flow swiftly to thee, and in thee never end.

Index of First Lines